Michel van der Stel M.A. The possibilit

Michel van der Stel

The

possibilities

of

the

connected

child

Michel van der Stel M.A. The possibilities of the connected child

www.michelvanderstel.com

Contents

Connect 28 January 2008...7

Untouched 30 January 1991..8

On the first sign of spring this year 8 February 2011 9

Pensive thought 27 February 2006....................................11

Supermarkets 5 March 1991 12

Thank you 7 March 2006..15

Collector's items 12 March 1991.......................................16

Carry 15 March 2011 18

Public Transport Rotterdam 16 March 1992 19

Trip 23 March 1995...21

Words away 8 April 2008 22

Clean 9 April 1991..25

Thoughts conceived in a free state 15 April 2004 27

Rubber? Pebble? 24 April 2006 29

English mint 6 May 1992..31

May & June 1991...33

The father play 7 June 1993...37

Name 5th July 1994 40

Paris 12 July 2011...43

Skin sensation 15 July 2010 46

Bleed me 1 August 2009 49

Amsterdam 6 August 2010 52

Torrent Affairs 19 August 1991 55

Pc 24 August 1993..57

Unfinished poem 24 August 2009.....................................59

What was going on in my living room at around 8 pm,
and before walking Boris the dog 6 November 1996 62

November Storms Anchored 9 November 2007.............64

Jangling sounds 27 November 1991 66

Instant 29 November 2010..67

Happy abandonment 18 December 2009........................70

She lets me in 21 December 2010 72

In loving memory of mum & dad

Connect 28 January 2008

And oftentimes clarity
Would come with the blink of an eye
A momentary lucid vision
A view without its trappings
No pomp
No circumstance
No frills
A transparent scene
Connect the dots connected
Meaning in every movement
One Aha Erlebnis
After another
And another
Eureka!
From the DNA-core
To the split ends
Really

Untouched 30 January 1991

The river's patched with icy clots
Light and subtle colour changes
Protected by the reedy fence
Haphazardly near the banks
No child yet placed a foot
Or threw a brick
Or branch of wood
To test the river's strength
Stretched mirror on the earth
Cutting sharply through the farmlands
On which the life stock grows
Vegetates
The frost of nights and days
To come
Did not secure the layer of ice
Not yet
Have patience
For the frost will burn the sun
Out of its welkin place
Extreme cold will take that place
Midnight
Thin fragile
This side up
Untouched
By the fingers of a growing child

On the first sign of spring this year 8 February 2011

The long absent sun
Makes everyone
Beautiful
The father who's biking the
Roundabout with his son
On his right arm
The girls with their winter hats
Who just exit the Polish supermarket
The big guy on his moped who's
Wearing the rastafarian colours on
His gloves
Even the trashy fat people
Look beautiful in this
Natural &
Strong solar light
I love them all & feel at
Ease
Cycling home to my new found
Love's house
I realise that I'm getting to
Know the neighbourhood by now
& I'm starting to recognise the
Men & women & children that
Populate it
My Vietnamese grocery store owner
Knows me by name & always shows her
Pleasant smile &
As I'm picking up my weekly order
Of organic veggies & fruit she is

Teaching two young trainee girls
How to do it
Smile
Reflection of old Sol
A Turkish neighbour
Sat himself down on the
Wooden bench that is outside
Our house &
His only occupation at this moment
As I'm approaching the door to
The house on my bike
Is to let the sun's rays touch his
Face
It is a bearded & moustached face
With pleasant eyes &
Topped with a beige hat like a fez
But not a fez
He is eager to share his fun in
The sun &
Finds in me a fellow admirer
We understand & connect in that
Brief moment that we show our love
In words
He smiles as he talks to me & I
Do the exact same
My world is filled with love &
Beauty &
Sun

Pensive thought 27 February 2006

The snowcovered fields
Murmur peace
Yet who is there to hear
When the hustle and the
Bustle of the big city
Over there
Drown out the faint sounds
The white blanket covered
Meadows make
Prick up your ears and listen
Carefully for it is the Lord
Shiva who calls us to unity
Listen to the murmur of the
Fields chanting their repetitive
One one one
It is there within our audio reach
If only we cared to be silent and listen
For a little while

Supermarkets 5 March 1991

Lots of pieces must have been
Written
On supermarkets I'm sure
Not newspaper articles
Or commercial leaflets
Nay
High & lofty literature
With the cliche capital L
Poems prose & what have you
Heck even plays I think
Lots of pieces written
On such an ideal setting
- Yes Mr Silk of course we
Do sell milk
Several brands
Several tastes & qualities
Nowhere cheaper –
Lots of
Rice soup candy cosmetics
Dogfood
So good
Vegetables in cans glass
Meat very neat meat
Oh where are all those
Pieces…
Everyone's familiar with the turf
- Now at your local supermarket
White beans in tomato sauce
15 p. only –

No social barrier
No obligation to buy
The shopper is saint
Customer king
& I who work there
A commoner
To serve honour & obey
The boss
Survive
The rotten giro at the
End of the month
Who hasn't been in a supermarket
Even songs exist like
"When I went to the supermarket"
"After I put some eggs in my basket"
"Supermarket boogie"
Supermarket Blues
Never been?
I don't believe c'mon
Never?
The smallest baby has…
Who are you trying to…
Cut it out
Rows of sugar packs
Salt &
All the spices on a special
Shelf
Where housewives kill their
Time
Where I kill time
Exchange it rather for that

Giro goddamn giro
What about the rows of tills
With lighted numbers on a pole
& silly women sitting there
Silly women buying there
Lots of pieces
Yes I'm sure…

Thank you 7 March 2006

You!
You teach me patience and control
When all I want to do is be
Impatient and out of control
You show me that you have
Self-constraint
Thereby teaching me a noble
And worthy lesson
How can I constrain
Myself
When I know
You're there
Within reach
How do you constrain yourself?
I do not get it my dear
Yet because you do
I
Have to
Forced by you
You teach me
To wait
And work on my virtues
And I have to
Thank you for that
So here it goes:
Thank you

Collector's items 12 March 1991

It's not a matter of making it
Understandable
Or to simplify
Hell no
Not a chosen method
Premeditated action
Yet I cannot use the terms
Organic
Natural
Innate
The way it grew up or
Out to be
For although I do not
Mind a linkage with
Romanticism
Wordsworth
Shelley & all those
Scribblers who put the
I eye aye first
And dotted it all over
With sentimental
Sentiments
It does not describe it in
An adequate way
I cannot put a finger on it
Even if all ten are used
In short every other
Terminology one
Feels apt to use

To label me or
To label it with (for it &
I are interchangable but
At the same time complementary)
Will not succeed in
Covering the whole picture
Touching every detail
Every seemingly insignificant
Part particle etc
Down to the terms of
Chemistry
Where atoms & the parts
Of atoms…
It's not restrictive
Ruling out
Rather rules are out
So ruling everything in
Every dot sigh leave
& I see you thinking
Down the wornout paths
Trodding where so many have
& still I do
Not have even the smallest
Inkling
To call it goD
To be continued yessir

Carry 15 March 2011

The day is filled with
A crispy newness
Tangible
I step a careful step
& try not to crush it underneath
My feet
As I walk barefoot through
The labyrinth
The perpetually moving
Maze that is all around me
I whistle & hum & attempt a
Tune that I can carry
Seeking contentment on this
Spring day in March
Another new day
Filled with possibilities

Public Transport Rotterdam 16 March 1992

I'm sensitive to all the odours
Fragrances & smells that live &
Multiply the subway maze
The stench of perfume
Overwhelming a chained
Series of farts from a wild-
Bearded bald boozer with a
Plastic bag belling
Empty bottles
The suffocating warmth of
The carriages where temperatures are
Kept high until July to kill the bugs &
Drown the harder smells of
Puke & baby diapers
Bad breath &
Smoking passengers
A 15 minute trip can mean
Maroc cocaine or just
Tobacco any kind
Most unkind
Come summertime the
Heat & smells become
Unbearable – be the
Windows ope or not
I love my city's
Tube the underground &
Aboveground lines
The peculiar smell of
Old men – above seventy –

A mix of piss & after shave
Cigars & cheap liquor
A dog with gas
The vomit of a drunk
The underground is full of it
Public Transport Rotterdam

Trip 23 March 1995

For the first time since I don't know
My mum is going on a holiday
Alone
Well as good as
For these years' acquaintance
Of kindergarten
My time
Is accompanying her
To the north of Spain
I just read in the National
Book week gift of L. De Winter
That by this trip she will be burying
My father after '93
His final burial
But will this be so in my mother's case?
I'll await the possible change that
Will occur after August 95 when she
Will have made the trip by coach
Or was it by plane?
Nay, by coach I think

Words away 8 April 2008

The words crawl out of my warm moist soft mouth
Over my lips and paper tongue struggling using
both arms
All of them
Their faces disturbed distorted and dismayed
Inconsistency in their motion
- they do and they don't want to leave the
Security of their origins
To venture out into the dark and deafening world
A world that they will partially undo of one of
Its qualities
The words will undeafen
I think they are my pets my cuddly furry friends
My smooth skinned creepy crawlies
My buzzing bees and skitling bugs
A Noah am I
They are alive and purposeful
They are alive and meaningless
They are alive and matter
Sometimes
They do
Not
My sweet sweet words always
Companions
For all time
Yet
Some
Times
They

Have no desire at all to stay
Away away
Find the nooks and crannies
To flee through
Some dumber words
Splatter and splash and splat
Against my windows
Leaving greasy slimy stains
That take forever to clean
Ending up as tinny puddles on
My window sill
The lighter words as bubbles are
Blown by a child on a breezeless
Summer's day in early May
Their light and soapy features mock gravity and
Show pretty prism pictures when the sunlight hits
Them quite intentionally
And they – the lighter words – seek out the cracks
and
Cuts in my ceiling
Away away
The hardest part is letting go
I burb them out and off they go
I send them forth they're on their own
I give release and deny
Responsibility for their actions
Minds of their own
Not mine
If ever they were
Yet secretly I am a proud father
Of all my words

I wish them well
With high hopes
For the best
For the rest of
Their natural
Lives

Clean 9 April 1991

The bloodstained syringe
Points the shortest way
To the station where the
Trains will run to Central
& to the suburbs going in
Reverse
I will not
Reverse
A sixty-3 year old man
Who rode a bike
A bicycle
Was run down
Yesterday's heroes
Who shoveled the dust
The broken stones
Broken bones
A broken needle
There was a song &
Now they adapted the
Title 4
We are entitled
Clean up our neighbourhood
Coming Thursday it'll be my
Street my very own
Visited by men in orange
Overalls
Cleaning up what's on the
Streets the shit &
Paper wrappers & puke &

Thereby emphasising underlining
Stressing
Do I make myself clear
The dirt that's real & in
The street that is
The street
I clean my hands
A full time job

Thoughts conceived in a free state 15 April 2004

For almost five whole hours
On a Wednesday afternoon
In the month of April my
Whole universe comprises
Of a small cubicle which
Is no bigger than a cell
In a penitentary
Facility anywhere
In the civilised world where
We discuss the concept of
Freedom

I do not exist outside
My womb my refuge haven
There is no meaning no truth
Reality is within
The interaction I have
Out there is surreal dreamlike
Removed from the inner truth
And limited I conclude
To the bare necessities
Of human interface
And smiles

From three dissimilar wells
The worded thoughts spin like a
Counter clockwise coherent
Separate current in a
Maelstrom that whirls with time

One well stronger and louder
Than the others entwining
Two and one well distinctly
Different embracing the two
In similar fashion the
Third

Oral strings of DNA
Building life and synergy
Creators of a value
That's priceless beyond compare
Thoughts become alive in here
Words are live and live
In my cubicled safe world
Where I co-control the flow
The movement and the action
My input is essential
Here

For five small hours I feel that
There is a purpose and a
Goal a higher truth above
The dairy drab of hapless
And evenly paced routine
I thrive in this confined state
Of human beings thinking
Talking sharing daring yet
I fully realise that
This too shall pass disolve and
Fade…

Rubber? Pebble? 24 April 2006

See the young budding artist
Struggle to make even the slightest dent
Upon the world around him
Through his art and his role as the
Artist
All the while the same questions echoing
Through the crevices of his mind
When does art ever make an
Impact upon anything?
And...
To top up that question with another
What is art?
He would like to believe in the
Pebble in the brook theory
You know
The ripples in the form of circles
Start small from the epicentre
And then slowly but surely
Widen until they
Almost invisibly definitely very faintly
Touch the banks
Touch every object in the brook
The key word here being (of course)
Touch
Yet he oftentimes has the feeling that
Each and all around him have
A rubberlike quality
That although easily bent out of shape
Bounces back and regains its original

Form
As if nothing not a thing
Touched impressed made a
Difference
And so the young artist
Let's call him Henry
Loses his youth
Loses his buds
During the diligent output nay
Steady and prolific
Output
Until…
The output
Stops
And now
Dear reader
I would like you to
Ponder this
Question
Did Henry's art
Impact
Henry?

English mint 6 May 1992

Unnatural
Most unnatural
Created God
Lord who wore his long
(No mention beard)
Sad real sad
Scream for attention
Such a boy – a good 'un
Perhaps – punk cycles past
Waste watch wasted
Way of decent
Honesty
(If only you knew)
A role of mint
"From England all the
Way"
I accepted though
The size of a mint's
Too big (for her small &
Sober mouth she blabbed)
She passed it on to me
I took a mint &
A question whether I
Liked mints
Two ladylike
Ladysome women
OAPs
English mint & hair &
The sunny spell as topics for the day

A busstop
Revelation
In rural country
Made

May & June 1991

They sure could need new Noahs here
In cyclone-battered Bangladesh
Before the waters came
Running water cold & warm
For dishes showers baths or washing
Machines
The choppers of the West pour down
Aid in boxes wooden boxes
That splinter on impact with
The surface muddy surface
Where clusters of people have
Their roots ankle & knee -
Deep in the water
Neptune's will
Captured by the cameras of
BBC & CNN & other letters three
Making us donate still further parts
Of chip chip chipped off
Consciences
Where the irregular beating of
The President & this just in
Are intersparsed with Campari
Supper cookers & hotels
Before the waters came
The fields where rice seeds
Were planted were flooded by
More minor hands
& the right shoulder of
All-India never made

Bold lines of Western print
With the coming of each
Fresh cyclone
The value of Bangladesh
Dhakka
Relevant news
Fades
To a rare spot
On a news show late
& the middle pages
Paper pages of
The morning
Where this hour
The news is of
Another tribe
Where the water
Has come
The blood &
Perspiration
Counterweight for
Autonomy
Democracy
Free press
Haha
Fooled again
A proud nation nay people
Battered with words
Poison gas &
"real live ammo"
To again fade in
The big back of minds

The universal back of mind
Controlled by…
Where Kirkurk &
Sounds sharing samelike
Strength
Mosul
Sulamanya
Diyabakir
Are bastions
Of a five-fold suppression
Where 1949 and later
71 are numbers sacred
Held in high esteem
Although many old men &
Women way past 71 will
Never see their universal right
When words are followed up
By inadequate action
Not to go against the superpowers'
Grain
And children dying refugees
With diarrhoea
Mystery illnesses &
Cholera
Before the waters come
Oh Barzani
Reindeer &
Snow that varies sixteen
Times
Pure white dirty white
Gray powder strong

Iced etc perhaps
Snow mobiles stripe the
Scenery &
Fire's made the
Natural way no
Camping gaz
In Northern Scandinavia
The Samis live & die & live
& speak their language
Swedish & Norwegians
Finns to name a few
So keen on drawing lines
On maps
The bigger chunk is mine
The frozen water melts
In cans in Sami camps

The father play 7 June 1993

Our meetings always strained
With us alike diversity
You moulded shaped &
Reshaped me
No distance-factor
Here applies
The influence grows grows
Grows
And if I were to use a
Metaphor or simile
I'd talk about the
Umbilical cord that
String of flesh
Bounding mother to child
Child to mother
Relatives
Father & son
And now you're in
Hospital
Dehydrated weak &
Old
With tubes sticking in you
Almost out of hope
No faith that will sustain you
But for the faith that we create
It's strange to see a fighter
About to throw the towel
It's strange to see a father
Afraid of what's to come

One who never did show fear
Now in childlike state again
& we must play the father now
We the relatives next of kin
It's we who must not give up hope
The fight is there for us to win
And we must play the father now

We never let our feelings show
Towards each other
I can't remember if we ever did
Say to one another I love you
Son I love you father
Yet all the time we know that
Love & that respect is there
In ample qualities in both of us for both of us
I hear him talk about me like
A father proud
But only when he thinks I'm out
Of reach to pick up the
Words that flatter
I must be strong he thinks
Just like my old man I must be
Strong
I know

I think about the times we played
A game of billiards together
He was still the father then
The father stern who not
Approves the good shots I make

But disapproves the ones I don't
I must be strong
He teaches me
I must be strong
Like him
The games of billiards & the talks
Small talks we have during the game
Form the summit of the relationship
For me

And now you're in hospital
I must be strong &
You must play the father for me
Because I love you dad

Name 5th July 1994

Do they find eachother?
Something my granny could have said
Subdued friendly
Whisper-like
With a tinge of a foreign
Accent
European no doubt
I looked up from
My book
Up towards the
Lady – Excuse me?
A friendly return a warm
Interaction between strangers
Again she put the question
Do they find eachother
The boy and the girl?
Books are about love & the
Search for love a path thwarted
By obstacles & angles & lots of
Horse manure
Books are about the most essential
Quest of man & its everfailing end
Boy meets girl etc
No
Abrupt & strong without
Delay
It's about a lunatics' asylum
Cuckoo's nest
The lady small & tanned

& upper middle class
Was thrown
By my reply
I had a chance
To take a closer look
Couldn't make up my mind
Whether the tanned skin
Was caused by the last days' rays
Or by inherited genetic material

She was walking the dog
Orange bow-tie around its neck
She asked my dog's name
I didn't lie & gave its name
Boris
Immediately she used her new
Possession to the fullest
Boris come here Boris good boy
Boris!
Boris this & Boris that
Give a person your name & give away
(Or give up) your individual state
Of mind attempt to reach temporary
Freedom of existence
I did not tell her my own but
Was happy to tell my dog's
Name
In some people's eyes that makes
Me a bastard

Not content with the amount of

Attention the little lady wanted
More
To have walked away then
Would have been a perfect
Interface between two souls searching
For self-acknowledgement
But no
The bitch wanted more
Thus ruining the perfection we had
Created
Shattering the crystal sphere we built
Into tiny splintered tears
The small talk grew to enormous proportions
The dog's age the current world cup
Football games
In which Holland reached the
Quarter finals beating Ireland's greens
Blah blah
Oh fuck
Please move away and
Let me read about the lunatics of
This world

Paris 12 July 2011

From Rotterdam Central
To Paris Gare du Nord
By Thalys
8.58 am
Purple & red
Seat covers
Grey plastic siding &
Cheap panel
Lighting
Set the mood
For the
Marshland Lutetia &
Its promises of
Syrupy time &
Percolated coffee
We fly through the
Dutch landscape without
Delay for a mere
20 minutes it seems
Into Belgium
Upon arrival
Gare du Nord
The rain comes down
Hard
Upon the Paris in
Scene
Travellers being picked
Up by friends &
Husbands &

Uncles
Trolleys
Rattling on the
Platform
Metro to D'Italie & then
Porte Italie
Checking into the
Fully booked
Campanile Hotel
And then we walk
We walk towards
The river
We walk and see
The sights
We walk through
The Louvre's buildings
We walk
We have a break
At one of the Irish
Pubs & down a
Pint of their best
Guinness
And sing Hotel California
Together with a friendly
Stranger
While a bigbelleyed
Frenchman stands on
The pavement smoking
A cigarette and watching
The Tour de France
On the telly in the

Pub
We have dinner
At the mosaiced
Floor restaurant
With the cocky
Waiter & the
Awful street musician
Playing trumpet but
Needing many more
Lessons

Skin sensation 15 July 2010

The beads of perspiration
Obey the laws of gravity
And trickle down from numerous
Countless pores
In the right direction
Because Newton's Laws
Of Physics –
All three –
And because the aforementioned laws of gravity
I sweat on the
Treadmill as I do
My cardio
As a dance
Quick & slow
To run my 5K
I sweat in the
Sauna sitting
On my big
Yellow towel
Both experiences are
Equally satisfying
Movement causes an effort
In the one
While
Simply sitting still causes
A similar effect
More effectively
As I sweat all over
& as I am wearing

Less clothing that
Covers me
I feel touched
Literally I am
Touched
My largest organ
Weighing in at roughly
Six pounds
Experiences a
Touching caused
By the appearance
Of the sweat
Pouring through
Heavenly
To be touched
Paradise
Touch me
Again & again
Cooling down with
The cold water
Shower &
The outside terrace
Sunbed
Again has my skin touched
By various other
Elements
My one desire is met
By sweat &
Cold water drops
& the warm rays of sunlight
& even by the drops of rain

That come down on
Me this afternoon
I have my eyes closed
& simply say a
Humble thank you
To whomever wants to hear
Me
Be it Gods
Or Newton's spirit
Or be it the natural
Elements could they listen
Thank
You!

Bleed me 1 August 2009

I seek the God of Death
In drink &
The following
Alcohol induced
Rushes of
States beyond
Control
Beyond fear &
Fright
Let it go
Escape its grip
A gentle kiss
On the cheek
And then
Snap
The neck
In one
Violent
Movement
Double handed
Action
Snap
Loud sounded
Snap
It stings
They bite
It itches
The night
Has stars

Milky way
And flashing lights
I seek the Destroyer
In nature
The leafs of my
Garden tree
Centre piece
The patterns
Shades of light
And lighter
Shades of dark
Contrast with the
Night
I seek my peace
Eternal from
The blood sucking
Insects
While they
Bleed me
In smallest
Amounts
And still
I seek
Relentlessly
A zealot
A fanatic
A true believer
I [active verb]
Son of a man
That never
Came to take

Me
Home

Amsterdam 6 August 2010

And then August finds me here
Sitting in the touristfilled centre
Sweat on my back and
In my armpits
Wearing my bright green
Shirt
Almost fluorescent
Of our nation's capital
I've just spent a very
Pleasant evening &
Night
Filled with skin
Sensation
With a friend
And now I'm
About to meet
Another friend who
Brings her friend
For a visit
We'll do coffee
Somewhere
I've biked through the
City for close to half an
Hour
Weesperzijde
Ceintuurbaan
Museumplein
Central station
Ate a banana for lunch

After a late breakfast in the
Sun
& go with what the world
Brings me
This wouldn't have been as much
Fun had this been planned
Tourists aplenty
Pigeons in the dozens eating
Everything
Including small pieces
Of banana
Note that I
Did not feed them
Looking at the
Strangers around
Listening as well to the
Murmur of multilangual
Chit chat
Cheers &
Cries
People dressed in
Summerwear
Long brown boots
Follow white-grey
Loafers
Sports shoes &
The mandatory
Sandals
Some people look
Puzzled
Not amazed as much as

Lost in a world they
Know & don't know
1.35 pm

Torrent Affairs 19 August 1991

The blood runneth not in the streets
Just the heavy marks
Of reddish-green
The Sovjet tanks of
Yanayev
Will some Moscovite
Repeat the
Standing-in-front-of-a-column-
Of-tanks-trick
Performed
At life's risk
At risk of life
With the passing of
Barely fourteen months
Should I lament
The spotted com
The world buzzes
News
I am buzzing
Pumping more of that
Natural high
Adrenalin
And I imagine that
Now – just past noon –
Old Michael's doing the same
A hurricane
Sweeping across
The USA
Meteorology

Sociology
Politicology
And off
To work

Pc 24 August 1993

In the early morning quiet
Virginal serenity
Between breakfast & lunch
The atmosphere is tranquil
I feel at ease
The dog has been walked
& fed &
Now is sleeping its light
Sleep
The radio turned off
As is the telly

Today this minute I hear
Only the slight dis-
Harmonious hum of the PC

I shaved & showered this
Dull and wet Tuesday morn'
Brave Timon of Greece
I often think of you
Duped & tricked
You took the right approach
But somewhat overdone dear
Boy
The dog
Which goes by the name of
Boris
Is whining for the outdoor
Live of trees & grass &

Bitches' piss & shit
For he is suffering from the
Annual rut (period of sexual
Excitement of male dog)

It's just the two of us really
Although we have more pets in
The home (mice & rabbits)
It's not even a quarter to 11
I'll check the mailbox in a
Minute

Unfinished poem 24 August 2009

There's beauty in an
Unfinished poem
Nothing rounded off
Nothing
Completed
The sense of fulfillment
Prolonged / extended indefinitely
No volta
No witty
Thoughtful
Conclusion
Nothing that will make you go
Aha now I understand that
Odd remark of the second
Stanza
An unfinished poem
Shows more
Kinship
With life
Than a finished one
Unless you have just
That
A finished one –
A finished life I mean
Rounded off with a little
Fulfilling final
Episode in which
Every loose end

Is tied up
Everything comes
Together
A jigsaw completed
Have you ever?
And then the sigh
Satisfying sigh of
Accomplishment
Have you?
And then a little
Sleep
I oftentimes want
To go for the
Unfinished poem
Having it
Keeping it an
Integral part
Of me
The words reverberating
In my head
Brooding on how to write
The next line
And the next
The lines to keep me
Company in my
Solitary cell
I would wrap some longer line
Around my neck &
Wear it as a
Pretty scarf
The shorter lines as

Armbands
The inbetween short and long
A necklace could be
Keeping me warm
Giving me
Joy
I could play with the
Lines as a
Small boy would
With his favourite
Toy
And not suppress this
Childlike smile
Upon my face
So here's to all
The unfinished poems
Of the world
Scribbled on
Notepads
Lying on
Bedstands
Hidden in
Executive
Briefcases
May you...

What was going on in my living room at around 8 pm, and before walking Boris the dog 6 November 1996

Summer drew its close
In autumn-late this
Year
And all accompanying
Signs
Were there
Blah blah leafs
Blah blah storms &
Rains – you know
And with the shortening
Of the days &
Waxing of the nights
The spirit aroused from
Its slumber
Manifests itself
Strong stronger
Stronger still
Demanding attention lots
And lots

Autumn draws it ope
Ever earlier it seems
The days of kite-flying
On the beach
Yet barely dry in
Memory's book – the
Ink I mean barely

Dry
The stamp / mark /
The seal
Or days with snail
Crawling hours when
Before I'd go out
Onto the street
For groceries or trip
To the city or…
Before whatever I'd
Put on my sunblock lotion
Factor 10 at least –
All over my uncovered
Flesh & I'd often
Put on a baseball cap
Of my favourite team
Almost obsessively
Avoiding a suntan
Let alone sunburn
Well at least I don't
Have to…
And living keeps me
Wondering
Amazed at what I do
& see
And wonders keep me
Living this life
Of
Multiplicity

November Storms Anchored 9 November 2007

We see the rainclouds
Touch
The meadows and the farmland
Heavy in certain places
While the radio plays real soft
We enjoy the morning drive
That brings us to our
Destination
The taste of pancakes still in
Their mouths
Even after a proper brushing of the
Teeth
At ease
At peace
And full of stories that
Need need need
To be shared with me
Tales of observation and
Wonder
And school and television and
Toys
I
Drop them off at the appropriate
Time
And start filling and killing my
Time
With a number of things
Such as
Grocery shopping

Reading a newspaper writing
Early burly christmas cards
And this
The location is an
Odd
One
My divorced wife's
Father's
Office
Where I've been given
Hospitable
Refuge from the storm and the
Cold
Hot coffee and a
Newspaper by my
Ex wife's
Mother
I am
In November
Storms
Anchored
Strong

Jangling sounds 27 November 1991

My value's not
In finance to be found
On Wall Street or in
London's City
Or even Beursplein 5
And although my own
Has a high styled
Architectural
WTC I
Humbly beg to differ &
Decline your gracious
Offer No
Financial value mine
I'd rather paint myself
Another value
Fitting for my chosen
Mode / mould
To ascertain the
Higher spheres & make some
Jangling sounds
Sounds having discord in
Their unity

Instant 29 November 2010

Just a mere three weeks ago
I met this dame in Delft
We danced we drank we
Touched
My lady Madonna
The band played all the covers from
Our teenage years
And she made me move to the beat
Without feeling too conscious of what I was
Doing i.e. dancing
I wasn't too awkwardly aware of
Rhythmically meandering my legs and arms
Dancing
We sang along with the words and had a constant
Grin on our faces
And all the while I was going
What a cute woman, what a positive
Radiating sexy lady
My Madonna
She placed my arms around her
When I was standing behind her
Watching the band
And my hands gently touched her
Belly
I smelled her hair and
Quietly placed a kiss on top of her head
Instantaneous good feeling
The taxi driver at Delft Central Station
Took us to the remote location of the

Party
When finally we retrieved the address
Which set the mood of the evening as
Light-hearted & fun
No signs whatsoever of the tension or the
Stress of a first date
Before we found the right location
However, Party centre Onder Ons
We walked in on an anniversary of
A couple where we were greeted
By dogs & what looked like a bouncer
More laughs exchanged
More kisses exchanged as the evening grew
The Turkish taxi driver was quite a character
Helpful & macho
For he did not like to be told by my date that
He should drive there & there
Wanting to drop us off at the swimming pool
Some half a mile or so from the actual spot
And now we have crossed the three-week mark
Three weeks in which we've spent lots of time
Together
In which we
Agreed in earnest & fun to go steady
In which we made sweet passionate
Love
In which we went for a walk in a marshy
Wetland
Went to one of Holland's top attractions for
Young & old filled with magic & fairy
Tales witches spell-bound trees red

Dancing shoes
Always dancing
In which we very much in love
Enjoy each other's company so
Carefully start to make plans for the near
Future
Together
It can all be so simple &
Good
When I'm in love

Happy abandonment 18 December 2009

This morning
Still dark
As I was walking towards
The shed that has my bike
On which I make my
Commute
After having listened to Bobby Goldboro's
Honey
It suddenly
Dawned
Upon me
And made me
Shriek out
OMG
I have
Abandonment issues
That would explain a lot
Now wouldn't it
It would explain
The neverending stream of
Tears
I cry whenever I see my
Three bright boys
It would explain why
I probably & most
Possibly
Feel each time I have
To leave them in the care
Of their mum that

I
Am abandoning them
In quite
A similar fashion
To how I have
Been abandoned by
My father and
My mother
At the tender age
Of ten
Something broke
Beyond repair
So tears for them
Are simultaneously
Tears for me
The bike ride on
The snow clad paths
To the city centre
Had my face touched
By the snow flakes
That found already
Wet cheeks when
They impacted
I am a
Happy man

She lets me in 21 December 2010

This first day of winter
2010
Finds me
In an ermine clad
Europe in a house
Not my own
Where love reigns
In between the
Artificial Christmas tree
And the homemade bed
Where the wooden floor
Has wear & tear
From children's feet
Running & skidding
And where the fire place
Embraces the candle cluttered
Blue plastic platter
Of which we light the candles one by
One
So that the wick flamed
Lights guide us
On our meditated paths
Towards our selves &
Each other
This is her house
The house that Eveline built
And to which she lovingly &
Symbolically
Gave me the key

I embrace her

Printed in Great Britain
by Amazon